"Dance
first.
Think
later."

618
RULES TO
LIVE BY

"Dance first. Think later."

Kathryn & Ross Petras

WORKMAN PUBLISHING · NEW YORK

Library of Congress Cataloging-in-Publication Data is
available.

ISBN 978-0-7611-6170-7

Workman books are available at special discounts when
purchased in bulk for premiums and sales promotions
as well as for fund-raising or educational use. Special
editions or book excerpts also can be created to
specification. For details, contact the Special Sales
Director at the address below or send an email to
specialmarkets@workman.com.

Workman Publishing Company, Inc.
225 Varick Street
New York, NY 10014-4381
workman.com

WORKMAN is a registered trademark of Workman
Publishing Co., Inc.

Printed in the United States of America
First printing March 2011

10 9 8 7

INTRODUCTION

HOW SHOULD ONE LIVE LIFE?

Could you answer that question in one sentence or two?

One night, we were watching TV and saw David Letterman ask rocker Warren Zevon— who was diagnosed with terminal cancer at age 55—what he'd learned about life and death.

"Enjoy every sandwich," Zevon said.

That totally knocked us out.

The idea was refreshingly honest and unashamedly simple, yet deep. All too often in this rushing world, we're harangued with "practical" advice about money or success or getting ahead. And we lose sight of the big picture. The big picture expressed by Warren Zevon in one small phrase.

Enjoy every sandwich.

The phrase got us looking for other, equally pithy but profound rules to live by.

In your hands, you're holding the result of our search—618 nuggets of big picture wisdom. Street-smart insights from poker pros and insightful observations from poets. Quirky truths from comedians and evidence-based truths from scientists. Secrets of success from business moguls and secrets of enlightenment from philosophers. *"Dance First. Think Later."* is packed with knowledge culled from writers and speakers who range far and wide but share one common characteristic: They know how to live life well.

We hope you enjoy this book.

And, of course, we hope you remember to enjoy every sandwich.

—*Kathryn & Ross Petras*

The first and great commandment is: Don't let them scare you.

—ELMER DAVIS
WRITER

Sing in the shower. Dance to the radio. Tell stories. Write a poem to a friend, even a lousy poem. Do it as well as you possibly can. You will get an enormous reward. You will have created something.

—KURT VONNEGUT
WRITER

Rule No. 3

Never make a credit decision on a beach.

—VICTOR J. BOSCHINI
COLLEGE ADMINISTRATOR

Rule No. 4

Believe in life!

—W.E.B. DU BOIS
*SOCIOLOGIST/CIVIL RIGHTS
ACTIVIST, IN "LAST MESSAGE
TO THE WORLD"*

Rule No. 5

Do not wait for the Last Judgment. It takes place every day.

—ALBERT CAMUS
WRITER

Rule No. 6

Don't panic.

—Douglas Adams
WRITER

Rule No. 7

If you're alone in the kitchen and you drop the lamb, you can always just pick it up. Who's going to know?

—Julia Child
CHEF

Rule No. 8

Be kind, for everyone you meet is fighting a great battle.

—IAN MACLAREN
WRITER

Rule No. 9

Do stuff you will enjoy thinking about and telling stories about for many years to come. Do stuff you will want to brag about.

—RACHEL MADDOW
POLITICAL COMMENTATOR

Rule No. 10

The only dream worth having . . . is to live while you're alive and die only when you're dead.

—ARUNDHATI ROY
ACTIVIST/WRITER

Rule No. 11

"It depends" is almost always the right answer in any big question.

—LINUS TORVALDS
SOFTWARE ENGINEER

Rule No. 12

Spend the afternoon. You can't take it with you.

—ANNIE DILLARD
WRITER

Rule No. 13

Remember, you don't owe anybody any explanations, you don't owe your parents any explanations, you don't owe your professors any explanations.

—BONO
MUSICIAN/ACTIVIST

Rule No. 14

Laugh. Laughter is immeasurable. Be joyful though you have considered all the facts.

—WENDELL BERRY
WRITER/FARMER

Rule No. 15

If you can't get what you wish for, forget about it.

—**ANTONIO PIERRO**
WORLD WAR I VETERAN

Rule No. 16

Don't forget that some things count more than other things.

—WILLIAM SAROYAN
WRITER

Rule No. 17

Create a posse of dead people. Create an entourage of heroes. Put their pictures on your wall, and keep them in your mind.

—DAVID BROOKS
COLUMNIST

Rule No. 18

A little money helps, but what *really* gets it right is never— I repeat— *never* under any condition face the facts.

—RUTH GORDON
ACTRESS/WRITER

Rule No. 19

Never refuse a chance to sit down. And never refuse an opportunity to relieve yourself.

—EDWARD,
DUKE OF WINDSOR

Rule No. 20

Nothing important was ever accomplished without chutzpah. Columbus had chutzpah. The signers of the Declaration of Independence had chutzpah. Don't ever aim your doubt at yourself. Laugh at yourself, but don't doubt yourself.

—ALAN ALDA
ACTOR

Rule No. 21

Always be on the lookout for the presence of wonder.

—E. B. WHITE
WRITER

Rule No. 22

Never trust someone who can't eat a meal alone at their own kitchen table.

—ELLEN BARKIN
ACTRESS

Rule No. 23

Breathe. Let go. And remind yourself that this very moment is the only one you know you have for sure.

—OPRAH WINFREY
MEDIA MAGNATE

Rule No. 24

Just because you like Jimi Hendrix doesn't mean you can play like Jimi Hendrix.

—ANTHONY BOURDAIN
CHEF

Rule No. 25

Never spend money before you have it.

—THOMAS JEFFERSON
STATESMAN

Rule No. 26

No matter how big or soft or warm your bed is, you still have to get out of it.

—GRACE SLICK
SINGER

Rule No. 27

Start where you are.
Use what you have.
Do what you can.

—ARTHUR ASHE
TENNIS PLAYER

Rule No. 28

If you don't get what you want, it's a sign either that you did not seriously want it, or that you tried to bargain over the price.

—RUDYARD KIPLING
WRITER

Rule No. 29

Work hard each day.

—"Rainbow Rule"
POSTED IN MRS. FOLTZ'S
FIRST-GRADE CLASS,
WATERBORO ELEMENTARY
SCHOOL, EAST WATERBORO,
MAINE

Rule No. 30

Never practice two vices at once.

—TALLULAH BANKHEAD
ACTRESS

Rule No. 31

When you see a good move, look for a better one.

—EMANUEL LASKER
CHESS MASTER

Rule No. 32

Live your life the way you want. You'll figure it out.

—JOHN GRISHAM
WRITER

Rule No. 33

Never kick a fresh turd on a hot day.

—HARRY S. TRUMAN
STATESMAN

Rule No. 34

Let the world know
you as you are,
not as you think
you should be,
because sooner
or later, if you are
posing, you will
forget the pose,
and then where
are you?

—FANNY BRICE
COMEDIAN

Rule No. 35

Better to do a little well than a great deal badly.

—SOCRATES
PHILOSOPHER

Rule No. 36

Question everything! You never know where a "silly question" may lead you.

— **DEREK ABBOTT**
*PHYSICIST/ELECTRONIC
ENGINEER*

Rule No. 37

We are all bozos on the same bus, so we might as well sit back and enjoy the ride.

— **WAVY GRAVY**
CLOWN/ACTIVIST

Rule No. 38

If you obey all the rules, you miss all the fun.

—KATHARINE HEPBURN
ACTRESS

Rule No. 39

Unless you have a hundred unanswered questions in your mind, you haven't read enough.

—DANIEL J. BERNSTEIN
*MATHEMATICIAN/
PROGRAMMER*

Rule No. 40

Dance first. Think later. It's the natural order.

—SAMUEL BECKETT
WRITER

Rule No. 41

Life is half delicious yogurt, half crap, and your job is to keep the plastic spoon in the yogurt.

—SCOTT ADAMS
CARTOONIST

Rule No. 42

If you wish to be a writer, write.

—EPICTETUS
GREEK PHILOSOPHER

Rule No. 43

You can't build a reputation on what you intend to do.

—LIZ SMITH
GOSSIP COLUMNIST

Rule No. 44

Live as if you were already living for a second time and as if you had made the mistakes you are about to make now.

—VIKTOR FRANKL
PSYCHIATRIST

Rule No. 45

Trust everyone, but always cut the cards.

—BENNY BINION
CASINO OPERATOR

Rule No. 46

If you intend to go to work, there is no better place than right where you are.

—ABRAHAM LINCOLN
STATESMAN

Rule No. 47

Once you can accept the universe as matter expanding into nothing that is something, wearing stripes with plaid comes easy.

—ALBERT EINSTEIN
PHYSICIST

Rule No. 48

Follow your passion, stay true to yourself. Never follow anyone else's path, unless you're in the woods and you're lost and you see a path, and by all means you should follow that.

—Ellen DeGeneres
COMEDIAN/TALK SHOW HOST

Rule No. 49

Don't be afraid of
missing opportunities.
Behind every failure is
an opportunity somebody
wishes they had missed.

—JANE WAGNER
WRITER/DIRECTOR

Rule No. 50

If you have only one smile
in you, give it to the people
you love. Don't be surly
at home, then go out in the
street and start grinning
"Good morning" at total
strangers.

—MAYA ANGELOU
WRITER

Rule No. 51

When angry, count four; when very angry, swear.

—MARK TWAIN
WRITER

Rule No. 52

The boss is never your friend, even if you're sleeping with him.

—JACOB M. APPEL
PLAYWRIGHT

Rule No. 53

Take it easy, but take it.

—WOODY GUTHRIE
FOLKSINGER

Rule No. 54

If you have an important point to make, don't try to be subtle or clever. Use a pile driver. Hit the point once. Then come back and hit it again. Then hit it a third time—a tremendous whack.

—WINSTON CHURCHILL
STATESMAN

Rule No. 55

Never tell people how you are. They don't want to know.

—JOHANN WOLFGANG
VON GOETHE
WRITER

Rule No. 56

Stop eating while still hungry and do not continue until you are satisfied.

—SAINT JOHN CASSIAN
MYSTIC

Rule No. 57

Certainly the game is rigged. Don't let that stop you; if you don't bet, you can't win.

—LAZARUS LONG
*CHARACTER IN WRITER
ROBERT A. HEINLEIN'S
"FUTURE HISTORY"
SCIENCE FICTION SERIES*

Rule No. 58

It's not what you are that counts, it's what they *think* you are.

—ANDY WARHOL
ARTIST

Rule No. 59

If you can't dazzle them with brilliance, baffle them with bull.

—W. C. FIELDS
COMEDIAN

Rule No. 60

Don't be humble. You're not that great.

—GOLDA MEIR
STATESWOMAN

Rule No. 61

Keep fightin' for freedom and justice, beloveds, but don't you forget to have fun doin' it. Lord, let your laughter ring forth. Be outrageous, ridicule the fraidy-cat, rejoice in all the oddities that freedom can produce. And when you get through kickin' ass and celebratin' the sheer joy of a good fight, be sure to tell those who come after how much fun it was.

—MOLLY IVINS
WRITER

Rule No. 62

If you liked a book, don't meet the author.

—RAYMOND CHANDLER
WRITER

Rule No. 63

Don't long for the unripe grape.

—HORACE (QUINTUS HORATIUS FLACCUS)
ROMAN POET

Rule No. 64

Don't take any of it too seriously.

—CHER
SINGER/ACTRESS

Rule No. 65

Life is short—avoid causing yawns.

—ELINOR GLYN
WRITER

Rule No. 66

Never let your sense of morals get in the way of doing what's right.

—Isaac Asimov
WRITER

Rule No. 67

Do not be concerned with escaping safely.

—BRUCE LEE
MARTIAL ARTS MASTER

Rule No. 68

You don't save a pitcher for tomorrow. Tomorrow it may rain.

—LEO DUROCHER
BASEBALL MANAGER

Rule No. 69

Truth is always exciting. Speak it, then. Life is boring without it.

—PEARL S. BUCK
WRITER

Rule No. 70

Don't carry a grudge. While you're carrying the grudge, the other guy's out dancing.

—BUDDY HACKETT
COMEDIAN/ACTOR

Rule No. 71

It's the way you play that
makes it. What I say is,
for Christ's sake, you don't
have to kill yourself to swing.
Play like you play. Play like
you think, and then you got
it, if you're going to get it.
And whatever you get, that's
you, so that's your story.

—COUNT BASIE
MUSICIAN

Rule No. 72

Don't hang a dismal picture on the wall. . . . Don't be a cynic and disconsolate preacher. Don't bewail and bemoan.

—RALPH WALDO
EMERSON
ESSAYIST

Rule No. 73

If everything is under control, you are going too slow.

—MARIO ANDRETTI
RACE CAR DRIVER

Rule No. 74

Stay home when you are drunk.

—EURIPIDES
PLAYWRIGHT

Rule No. 75

Ease up on yourselves. Have some compassion for yourself as well as for others. There's no such thing as perfection, and life is not a race.

—DOUG MARLETTE
CARTOONIST

Rule No. 76

Keep your old love letters.
Throw away your old bank
statements.

—MARY SCHMICH
COLUMNIST

Rule No. 77

Don't expect to be popular.
The better you do the job,
the more likely you are to
go against conventional
wisdom, and people don't
like to hear bad news.
So you are not going
to be popular.

—DAVID HALBERSTAM
JOURNALIST

Rule No. 78

Reason well from the beginning and then there will never be any need to look back with confusion and doubt.

—TENZIN GYATSO
14TH DALAI LAMA

Rule No. 79

Never be the first to arrive at a party or the last to go home, and never, ever be both.

—DAVID BROWN
MOVIE PRODUCER

Rule No. 80

Life is like one big Mardi Gras. But instead of showing your boobs, show people your brain, and if they like what they see, you'll have more beads than you know what to do with.

—ELLEN DeGENERES
COMEDIAN/TALK SHOW HOST

Rule No. 81

Always give an autograph when somebody asks you.

—TOMMY LASORDA
BASEBALL MANAGER

Rule No. 82

Consult your friend on all things, especially on those that respect yourself. His counsel may then be useful where your own self-love might impair your judgment.

—LUCIUS ANNAEUS
SENECA
*ROMAN PHILOSOPHER/
STATESMAN*

Rule No. 83

You can't stay in your corner of the forest waiting for others to come to you. You have to go to them sometimes.

—A. A. Milne
WRITER

Rule No. 84

If anybody laughs at your idea, view it as a sign of potential success!

—JIM ROGERS
FINANCIER

Rule No. 85

Avoid clichés, avoid generalizations, find your own voice, show compassion, and ask the important questions.

—AMY TAN
WRITER

Rule No. 86

Fill yourself with silence, you will find life, And your body shall flourish upon earth.

—AMENEMOPE
EGYPTIAN SCRIBE

Rule No. 87

Let your soul do the singin'.

—MA RAINEY
SINGER

Rule No. 88

Nobody is always a winner, and anybody who says he is, is either a liar or doesn't play poker.

—AMARILLO SLIM
(THOMAS ALAN
PRESTON JR.)
POKER PLAYER

Rule No. 89

Always remember that you are absolutely unique.

Just like everyone else.

—MARGARET MEAD
ANTHROPOLOGIST

Rule No. 90

Choosing the lesser of two evils is still choosing evil.

—**JERRY GARCIA**
MUSICIAN

Rule(s) No. 91

Herzog's Rules

1. Be on time.

2. Bust your butt.

3. Play smart.

4. Have some laughs while you're at it.

—**WHITEY HERZOG**
BASEBALL MANAGER

Rule No. 92

Play not the Peacock, looking every where about you, to See if you be well Decked, if your Shoes fit well, if your Stockings sit neatly, and Cloths handsomely.

—TRANSCRIBED BY GEORGE WASHINGTON *FROM* 110 RULES OF CIVILITY & DECENT BEHAVIOUR IN COMPANY AND CONVERSATION *(MID-1600S–EARLY 1700S)*

Rule No. 93

If you're looking for wisdom, call your grandmother.

—ALICE HOFFMAN
WRITER

Rule No. 94

I have ten commandments. The first nine are, "Thou shalt not bore." The tenth is, "Thou shalt have right of final cut."

—BILLY WILDER
FILM DIRECTOR

Rule No. 95

Laughing at someone
else is an excellent
way of learning how
to laugh at oneself,
and questioning what
seem to be the absurd
beliefs of another
group is a good way
of recognizing the
potential absurdity
of many of one's own
cherished beliefs.

—GORE VIDAL
WRITER

Rule No. 96

The world is movement,
and you cannot be stationary
in your attitude toward
something that is moving.

—HENRI
CARTIER-BRESSON
PHOTOGRAPHER

Rule No. 97

If you're not in the parade,
you watch the parade.
That's life.

—MIKE DITKA
FOOTBALL COACH

Rule No. 98

Don't think. Thinking is the enemy of creativity.

—RAY BRADBURY
WRITER

Rule No. 99

Do not fear to be eccentric in opinion, for every opinion now accepted was once eccentric.

—BERTRAND RUSSELL
MATHEMATICIAN/
PHILOSOPHER

Rule No. 100

Don't be afraid of the truth.

—JOHN A. VUCETICH
PROFESSOR

Rule No. 101

If you don't feel like doing something, don't do it. My cardiologist told me that.

—RED AUERBACH
BASKETBALL COACH

Rule No. 102

Learning what you don't want to do is the next best thing to figuring out what you do want to do.

—ANDERSON COOPER
NEWS ANCHOR

Rule No. 103

The only time to eat diet food is while you're waiting for the steak to cook.

—JULIA CHILD
CHEF

Rule No. 104

Beware of all enterprises that require new clothes.

—HENRY DAVID
THOREAU
TRANSCENDENTALIST

Rule No. 105

If you have a garden and a library, you have everything you need.

—Marcus Tullius Cicero

ROMAN PHILOSOPHER/ STATESMAN

Rule No. 106

The number-one rule of the road is never go to bed with anyone crazier than yourself. You will break this rule, and you will be sorry.

—**KRIS KRISTOFFERSON**
MUSICIAN/ACTOR

Rule No. 107

Before you start some work, always ask yourself three questions: Why am I doing it? What will the results be? Will I be successful? Only when you think deeply and find satisfactory answers to these questions, go ahead.

—CHANAKYA
POLITICIAN KNOWN AS
THE INDIAN MACHIAVELLI

Rule No. 108

All suffering is caused by being in the wrong place. If you're unhappy where you are, *move*.

—TIMOTHY LEARY
*PROFESSOR/
COUNTERCULTURE ICON*

Rule No. 109

Sometimes you have to be a bitch to get things done.

—MADONNA
SINGER

Rule No. 110

If fate means you to lose, give him a good fight anyhow.

—WILLIAM MCFEE
WRITER

Rule No. 111

Whenever you have a little bit of time for yourself, read a book. Always carry something with characters written on it with you and look at it when no one's looking.

—HOJO SOUN
SAMURAI

Rule No. 112

Hold every moment sacred.

—THOMAS MANN
WRITER

Rule No. 113

Don't be afraid. Because you're going to be afraid. But remember when you become afraid, just don't be afraid.

—JOAN JETT
MUSICIAN

Rule No. 114

Never contend with a man who has nothing to lose.

—**Baltasar Gracián y Morales**
WRITER/PRIEST

Rule No. 115

Always, in all circumstances,
wear comfortable shoes.
You never know when you
may have to run for your life.

—CALLIE KHOURI
SCREENWRITER/DIRECTOR

Rule No. 116

If you don't fail at least 90
percent of the time, you're
not aiming high enough.

—ALAN CURTIS KAY
COMPUTER SCIENTIST

Rule No. 117

Never play checkers with a man who carries his own board.

—BRANCH RICKEY
BASEBALL MANAGER

Rule No. 118

Watch with glittering eyes the whole world around you, because the greatest secrets are always hidden in the most unlikely places.

—ROALD DAHL
WRITER

Rule No. 119

It's okay to be fat. So you're fat. Just be fat and shut up about it.

—ROSEANNE BARR
COMEDIAN

Rule No. 120

As long as you live, keep learning how to live.

—LUCIUS ANNAEUS
SENECA
*ROMAN PHILOSOPHER/
STATESMAN*

Rule No. 121

Avoid foolhardiness, do not attempt to match four or six opponents at once. Restrain your ambition, this will benefit you. It is no shame to flee from four or six.

—JOHANNES
LIECHTENAUER
FENCING MASTER

Rule No. 122

Tip generously. You go around only once, and tipping generously is a meaningful way to improve your own quality of life.

—DANNY MEYER
RESTAURATEUR

Rule No. 123

If you're going to be crazy, you have to get paid for it or else you're going to be locked up.

—HUNTER S. THOMPSON
JOURNALIST

Rule No. 124

Live like a mud-fish: its skin is bright and shiny even though it lived in mud.

—**RAMAKRISHNA**
BENGALI MYSTIC

Rule No. 125

If you say that there are elephants flying in the sky, people are not going to believe you. But if you say that there are four hundred and twenty-five elephants in the sky, people will probably believe you.

—GABRIEL GARCÍA MÁRQUEZ
WRITER

Rule No. 126

Don't ever forget two
things I'm going to tell
you. One, don't believe
everything that's written
about you. Two, don't pick
up too many checks.

—BABE RUTH
BASEBALL PLAYER

Rule No. 127

It's okay
to be wrong.

—DAVID HENRY HWANG
PLAYWRIGHT

Rule No. 128

Don't hold your parents up to contempt. After all, you are their son, and it is just possible that you may take after them.

—EVELYN WAUGH
WRITER

Rule No. 129

Something to think about: If you fish the wrong fly long and hard enough, it will sooner or later become the right fly.

—JOHN GIERACH
FLY FISHERMAN

Rule No. 130

Put all your eggs in one basket and watch the basket.

—Carl Sandburg
WRITER

Rule No. 131

You never want to give a man a present when you know he's feeling good. You want to do it when he's down.

—Lyndon B. Johnson
STATESMAN

Rule No. 132

Gamble everything for love, if you are a true human being.

—RUMI

PERSIAN POET/MYSTIC

Rule No. 133

The important thing is not to stop questioning; curiosity has its own reason for existing. One cannot help but be in awe when contemplating the mysteries of eternity, of life, of the marvelous structure of reality. It is enough if one tries merely to comprehend a little of the mystery every day. Never lose a holy curiosity.

—ALBERT EINSTEIN
PHYSICIST

Rule No. 134

Keep away from people who try to belittle your ambitions. Small people always do that, but the really great make you feel that you, too, can become great.

—MARK TWAIN
WRITER

Rule No. 135

Don't worry about people stealing an idea. If it's original, you'll have to ram it down their throats.

—HOWARD AIKEN
COMPUTER SCIENTIST

Rule No. 136

Love with your mouth shut, help without breaking your ass or publicizing it, keep cool but care.

—THOMAS PYNCHON
WRITER

Rule No. 137

It is fatal to look hungry. It makes people want to kick you.

—GEORGE ORWELL
WRITER

Rule No. 138

What's the old saying? "Don't look back; somebody might be catching up." Well, don't even slow down, much less look back.

—WILLIE NELSON
MUSICIAN

Rule No. 139

Don't cry because it's over, smile because it happened.

—Dr. Seuss
(Theodor Geisel)
WRITER

Rule No. 140

It pays to be obvious, especially if you have a reputation for subtlety.

—ISAAC ASIMOV
WRITER

Rule No. 141

Smoked carp tastes just as good as smoked salmon when you ain't got no smoked salmon.

—PATRICK F. MCMANUS
WRITER

Rule No. 142

Whenever you are asked if you can do a job, tell 'em, "Certainly, I can!" Then get busy and find out how to do it.

—THEODORE
ROOSEVELT
STATESMAN

Rule No. 143

Why not be oneself? That is the whole secret of a successful appearance. If one is a greyhound, why try to look like a Pekingese?

—EDITH SITWELL
WRITER

Rule No. 144

Take calculated risks. That is quite different from being rash.

— GEORGE S. PATTON
GENERAL

Rule No. 145

Don't have good ideas if you aren't willing to be responsible for them.

— ALAN JAY PERLIS
COMPUTER SCIENTIST

Rule No. 146

When I first started racing, my father, one of the first things he said, he said, "Win the race as slow as you can."

—RICHARD PETTY
RACE CAR DRIVER

Rule No. 147

If you want to grow old as a pilot, you've got to know when to push it and when to back off.

—CHUCK YEAGER
TEST PILOT

Rule No. 148

The three sentences that will get you through life:

Number one, "Cover for me."

Number two, "Oh, good idea, boss."

Number three, "It was like that when I got here."

—HOMER SIMPSON
CARTOON CHARACTER,
THE SIMPSONS

Rule No. 149

Have fun. And go home when you're tired.

—GEORGE ABBOTT
DIRECTOR/PRODUCER/
PLAYWRIGHT

Rule No. 150

If you end up with a boring miserable life because you listened to your mom, your dad, your teacher, your priest, or some guy on television telling you how to do your shit, then you deserve it.

—FRANK ZAPPA
MUSICIAN

Rule No. 151

It's not what happens to you, but how you react to it that matters.

—EPICTETUS
ROMAN PHILOSOPHER

Rule No. 152

Dare to be naive.

—R. BUCKMINSTER
FULLER
*ARCHITECT/DESIGNER/
INVENTOR*

Rule No. 153

Stick to your story. It is not the most important subject in history but it is one about which you are uniquely qualified to speak.

—EVELYN WAUGH
WRITER

Rule No. 154

Never run away from a gun. Bullets can travel faster than you can.

—WILD BILL HICKOCK
GUNFIGHTER/SCOUT

Rule No. 155

If you are praised, be silent. If you are scolded, be silent. If you incur losses, be silent. If you receive profit, be silent. If you are satiated, be silent. If you are hungry, also be silent. And do not be afraid that there will be no fruit when all dies down; there will be! Not everything will die down. Energy will appear; and what energy!

—SAINT FEOFIL
RUSSIAN MYSTIC

Rule No. 156

Don't ever ask anyone for an opinion of your performance. They're liable to tell you.

— **JERRY STILLER**
COMEDIAN

Rule No. 157

You should assume everything you read online is false until you can confirm it somewhere else.

— **JOHN STARK**
*SEC INTERNET
ENFORCEMENT CHIEF*

Rule No. 158

Never throw a long line when a short one will serve your purpose.

—RICHARD PENN
FISHERMAN

Rule No. 159

Be yourself; everyone else is already taken.

—OSCAR WILDE
WRITER

Rule No. 160

Remember: Upon the conduct of each depends the fate of all.

—**ALEXANDER THE GREAT**
GREEK RULER

Rule No. 161

A good hockey player plays where the puck is. A great hockey player plays where the puck is going to be.

—Wayne Gretzky
HOCKEY PLAYER

Rule No. 162

The big secret in life is that there is no big secret.

—Oprah Winfrey
MEDIA MAGNATE

Rule No. 163

Be daring, be different,
be impractical, be anything
that will assert integrity
of purpose and imaginative
vision against the play-it-
safers, the creatures
of the commonplace, the
slaves of the ordinary.

—CECIL BEATON
PHOTOGRAPHER

Rule No. 164

Get and stay out of your comfort zone. I believe that not much happens of any significance when we're in our comfort zone.

—BOB PARSONS
DIGITAL ENTREPRENEUR

Rule No. 165

Exposing money in a public place is pretty stupid.

—DOYLE BRUNSON
POKER PLAYER

Rule No. 166

Do not go to bed fearing tomorrow, For when day breaks what is tomorrow?

—AMENEMOPE
EGYPTIAN SCRIBE

Rule No. 167

Remember always that you have not only the right to be an individual, you have the obligation to be one. You cannot make any useful contributions in life unless you do that.

—ELEANOR ROOSEVELT
POLITICIAN/ACTIVIST

Rule No. 168

It is not enough to conquer; one must know how to seduce.

—Voltaire (François-Marie Arouet)
PHILOSOPHER

Rule No. 169

You have to learn how to duck, because they're gonna throw it at you.

—Arthur Miller
PLAYWRIGHT

Rule No. 170

The first rule of life is to have a good time. The second rule of life is to hurt as few people as possible. There is no third rule.

—BRENDAN GILL
WRITER

Rule No. 171

You have to grow from the inside out.

—VIVEKANANDA
BENGALI MYSTIC

Rule No. 172

Don't worry about mosquitoes
Don't worry about flies
Don't worry about insects in general

—F. SCOTT FITZGERALD
WRITER, TO HIS 11-YEAR-OLD DAUGHTER

Rule No. 173

Never murder a man who is committing suicide.

—WOODROW WILSON
STATESMAN

Rule No. 174

You must knock on doors until your knuckles bleed. Doors will slam in your face. You must pick yourself up, dust yourself off, and knock again. It's the only way to achieve your goals in life.

—MICHAEL USLAN
FILM PRODUCER

Rule(s) No. 175

The first rule is to keep an untroubled spirit.

The second is to look things in the face and know them for what they are.

—MARCUS AURELIUS
ROMAN EMPEROR

Rule No. 176

Be aware that most people are operating on a very condensed version of the Ten Commandments: the part about murder.

—MARK BRICKLIN
JOURNALIST

Rule No. 177

Be happy. It's one way of being wise.

—COLETTE
WRITER

Rule No. 178

Don't aim at success—the more you aim at it and make it a target, the more you are going to miss it. For success, like happiness, cannot be pursued; it must ensue, and it only does so as the unintended side-effect of one's personal dedication to a cause greater than oneself or as the by-product of one's surrender to a person other than oneself. Happiness must happen, and the same holds for success: you have to let it happen by not caring about it.

—VIKTOR FRANKL
PSYCHIATRIST

Rule No. 179

When people talk, listen
completely. Most people
never listen.

—ERNEST HEMINGWAY
WRITER

Rule No. 180

I understand that fear
is my friend, but not always.
Never turn your back on fear.
It should always be in front
of you, like a thing that
might have to be killed.

—HUNTER S. THOMPSON
JOURNALIST

Rule No. 181

If you judge people, you have no time to love them.

—MOTHER TERESA
HUMANITARIAN

Rule No. 182

There's only one way to become a hitter. Go up to the plate and get mad. Get mad at yourself and mad at the pitcher.

—TED WILLIAMS
BASEBALL PLAYER

Rule No. 183

Never pay any attention to what critics say. Remember, a statue has never been set up in honor of a critic!

—JEAN SIBELIUS
COMPOSER

Rule No. 184

Be warned against all "good" advice because "good" advice is necessarily "safe" advice, and though it will undoubtedly follow a sane pattern, it will very likely lead one into total sterility—one of the crushing problems of our time.

—JULES FEIFFER
CARTOONIST

Rule No. 185

If your only goal is to become rich, you will never achieve it.

—JOHN D.
ROCKEFELLER SR.
FINANCIER

Rule No. 186

When in doubt, make a fool of yourself. There is a microscopically thin line between being brilliantly creative and acting like the most gigantic idiot on earth. So what the hell, leap.

—CYNTHIA HEIMEL
WRITER/HUMORIST

Rule No. 187

Put yourself in their shoes before you decide on the best way to take their shirts.

—DAVID SKLANSKY
POKER PLAYER

Rule No. 188

Hit the ball over the fence and you can take your time going around the bases.

—JOHN W. RAPER
JOURNALIST

Rule No. 189

Never pass up the opportunity to have sex or be on television.

—GORE VIDAL
WRITER

Rule No. 190

Life is one big contradiction, and you'll drive yourself crazy if you try to figure it out. So don't.

—DIANE HALSTEAD
PROFESSOR

Rule No. 191

Enjoy every sandwich.

—**WARREN ZEVON**
*MUSICIAN, ON FACING
TERMINAL MESOTHELIOMA*

Rule No. 192

Study nature, love nature, stay close to nature. It will never fail you.

—**FRANK LLOYD
WRIGHT**
ARCHITECT

Rule No. 193

Whatever you can do, or dream you can, begin it. Boldness has genius, power and magic in it.

—JOHANN WOLFGANG
VON GOETHE
WRITER

Rule No. 194

You can never go home
again, but the truth is you
can never leave home,
so it's all right.

—MAYA ANGELOU
WRITER

Rule No. 195

If you got something
you don't want other
people to know, keep it
in your pocket.

—MUDDY WATERS
MUSICIAN

Rule No. 196

Don't underestimate the value of Doing Nothing, of just going along, listening to all the things you can't hear, and not bothering.

—A. A. MILNE
WRITER

Rule No. 197

Make a careful list of all things done to you that you abhorred. Don't do them to others, ever.

Make another list of things done for you that you loved. Do them for others, always.

—DEE HOCK
FOUNDER OF VISA

Rule No. 198

Do not conceive that fine clothes make fine men, any more than fine feathers make fine birds.

—GEORGE WASHINGTON
STATESMAN

<u>Rule No. 199</u>

Nothing that comes easy is worth a dime. As a matter of fact, I never saw a football player make a tackle with a smile on his face. Never.

—**WOODY HAYES**
COLLEGE FOOTBALL COACH

Rule No. 200

Shall we make a new rule of life from tonight: always to try to be a little kinder than is necessary?

—J. M. BARRIE
WRITER

Rule No. 201

If you can't be kind, at least be vague.

—MISS MANNERS
(JUDITH MARTIN)
ETIQUETTE EXPERT

Rule No. 202

The Linux philosophy is "laugh in the face of danger." Oops. Wrong one. "Do it yourself." That's it.

—LINUS TORVALDS
SOFTWARE ENGINEER

Rule No. 203

Screen credit is valuable only
when it's given you. If you're
in a position to give yourself
credit, you don't need it.

—IRVING THALBERG
FILM PRODUCER

Rule No. 204

Learn to draw. Or to play
the cello. Or to tap dance.
Something impractical, even
useless. Whatever it is, it
ought to be hard for you,
something you haven't really
got time for, and that by
professional standards you
probably won't ever do well.

—JOHN WALSH
ART HISTORIAN

Rule No. 205

Never invest short and borrow long.

—CHARLES SCHWAB
INVESTOR

Rule No. 206

Never memorize what you can look up in books.

—ALBERT EINSTEIN
PHYSICIST

Rule No. 207

What the hell— you might be right, you might be wrong . . . but don't just avoid.

—KATHARINE HEPBURN
ACTRESS

Rule No. 208

It is said an Eastern monarch once charged his wise men to invent him a sentence . . . which should be true and appropriate in all times and situations. They presented him the words: "And this, too, shall pass away."

—ABRAHAM LINCOLN
STATESMAN

Rule No. 209

Don't interrupt a man in the midst of being ironic, it's not polite.

—RAY BRADBURY
WRITER

Rule No. 210

Do your little bit of good where you are; it is those little bits of good put together that overwhelm the world.

—DESMOND TUTU
RELIGIOUS LEADER/ACTIVIST

Rule No. 211

Be not afraid of life. Believe that life is worth living, and your belief will help create the fact.

—WILLIAM JAMES
PSYCHOLOGIST/PHILOSOPHER

Rule No. 212

Stay Hungry.
Stay Foolish.

—STEVE JOBS
*APPLE COFOUNDER,
QUOTING THE FINAL
ISSUE OF* THE WHOLE
EARTH CATALOG *AS WORDS
THAT GUIDE HIS LIFE*

Rule No. 213

Never trust a man unless you've got his pecker in your pocket.

—LYNDON B. JOHNSON
STATESMAN

Rule No. 214

You got to look on the bright side, even if there ain't one.

—DASHIELL HAMMETT
WRITER

Rule No. 215

If you have the choice between humble and cocky, go with cocky. There's always time to be humble later, once you've been proven horrendously, irrevocably wrong.

—KINKY FRIEDMAN
SINGER/WRITER

Rule No. 216

The things to do are:
the things that need
doing, that *you* see need
to be done, and that
no one else seems
to see need to be done.
Then you will conceive
your own way of doing
that which needs to
be done—that no one
else has told you to do
or how to do it.

—R. BUCKMINSTER
FULLER
ARCHITECT/DESIGNER/
INVENTOR

Rule No. 217

Life is uncertain.
Eat dessert first.

—ERNESTINE ULMER
WRITER

Rule No. 218

Confront a corpse at least once. The absolute absence of life is the most disturbing and challenging confrontation you will ever have.

—DAVID BOWIE
MUSICIAN

Rule No. 219

It's always a good move to listen to that inner voice— if it doesn't lead to a crime.

—LISA KUDROW
ACTRESS

Rule No. 220

"How you play the game" is for college ball. When you're playing for money, winning is the only thing that matters. Show me a good loser in professional sports, and I'll show you a player I'm looking to trade to Oakland.

—LEO DUROCHER
BASEBALL MANAGER

Rule No. 221

Take no advice, including this.

—CARL SANDBURG
WRITER

Rule No. 222

Keep breathing.

—SOPHIE TUCKER
*ENTERTAINER, ON THE
KEY TO LONGEVITY*

Rule No. 223

If somebody's trying to
shut you up, sing louder
and, if possible, better.

— SALMAN RUSHDIE
WRITER

Rule No. 224

Never let the future disturb
you. You will meet it with
the same weapons of
reason which today arm
you against the present.

— MARCUS AURELIUS
ROMAN EMPEROR

Rule(s) No. 225

1. Control your destiny or someone else will.

2. Face reality as it is, not as it was or you wish it were.

3. Be candid with everyone.

4. Don't manage, lead.

5. Change before you have to.

6. If you don't have a competitive advantage, don't compete.

—JACK WELCH
BUSINESSMAN

Rule No. 226

To survive you often have to fight, and to fight you have to dirty yourself.

—GEORGE ORWELL
WRITER

Rule No. 227

It can be done!

—César Chávez
ACTIVIST

Rule No. 228

You'll never find a rainbow if you're looking down.

—Charlie Chaplin
ACTOR/DIRECTOR

Rule No. 229

My father said,
"When in doubt,
castle."

— KURT VONNEGUT
WRITER

Rule No. 230

Don't try to go too
fast. Learn your
job. Don't ever
talk until you
know what you're
talking about.

— SAM RAYBURN
POLITICIAN

Rule No. 231

Take care of speaking thoughtlessly; When a man's heart is upset, words travel faster Than wind and rain.

—AMENEMOPE
EGYPTIAN SCRIBE

Rule No. 232

Where large sums
of money are concerned,
it is advisable to trust
nobody.

—AGATHA CHRISTIE
WRITER

Rule No. 233

Use your good judgment
in all situations. There
are no additional rules.

—NORDSTROM'S
RULES FOR
EMPLOYEES

Rule No. 234

If you can't convince them, confuse them.

—**Harry S. Truman**
STATESMAN

Rule No. 235

The world is more malleable than you think and it's waiting for you to hammer it into shape.

—BONO
MUSICIAN/ACTIVIST

Rule No. 236

The best way to cheer yourself up is to try to cheer somebody else up.

—MARK TWAIN
WRITER

Rule No. 237

Loneliness is one of the best things in the world for you. You do something about it: read, for instance, all kind of things, make friends.

—SHELBY FOOTE
HISTORIAN/WRITER

Rule No. 238

Take time to deliberate, but when the time for action has arrived, stop thinking and go in.

—NAPOLEON
BONAPARTE
EMPEROR

Rule No. 239

A schoolmaster of mine long ago said: You can only learn from the second-raters. The first-raters are out of range; you can't see how they get their effects.

—RAYMOND CHANDLER
WRITER

Rule No. 240

Do not dare not to dare.

—C. S. LEWIS
WRITER

Rule No. 241

Keep the other person's well-being in mind when you feel an attack of soul-purging truth coming on.

—BETTY WHITE
ACTRESS

Rule No. 242

You gotta try your luck
at least once a day, because
you could be going around
lucky all day and not even
know it.

—JIMMY DEAN
*SAUSAGE MOGUL/
COUNTRY SINGER*

Rule No. 243

You can take a chance with
any man who pays his bills
on time.

—TERENCE
ROMAN PLAYWRIGHT

Rule No. 244

Go confidently in the direction of your dreams. Live the life you have imagined.

—HENRY DAVID
THOREAU
TRANSCENDENTALIST

Rule No. 245

Respect the natives.

—WERNER HERZOG
FILM DIRECTOR

Rule No. 246

Friends and good manners will carry you where money won't go.

—Margaret Walker
EDUCATOR

Rule No. 247

The truth is, everyone is going to hurt you. You just got to find the ones worth suffering for.

—BOB MARLEY
MUSICIAN

Rule No. 248

Hide your good deeds as well as your evil ones.

—BISHR AL-HAFI
SUFI ASCETIC

Rule No. 249

Trust that little voice in your head that says, "Wouldn't it be interesting if . . ." And then do it.

—DUANE MICHALS
PHOTOGRAPHER

Rule No. 250

Don't let nobody cosign for you.

—Evander Holyfield
BOXER

Rule No. 251

Never tell people *how* to do things. Tell them *what* to do and they will surprise you with their ingenuity.

—George S. Patton
GENERAL

Rule No. 252

Back Up Your Hard Drive.
What do I mean by that?
Although your life may
be cruising along smoothly,
I recommend that every
once in a while you stop
and envision a sudden
shipwreck occurring.
Then think, re-think and
remember what you would
really want to hold on to
if disaster should strike.

—LARRY BOCK
VENTURE CAPITALIST

Rule No. 253

Pay your dues.
For God's sake,
pay your dues.
Jesus. I see all
these people
who want to be
overnight stars,
and that is so bad.
It'll just screw
you up so badly.

—ALEX TREBEK
GAME SHOW HOST

Rule No. 254

If you are squeamish don't prod the beach rubble.

—SAPPHO
POET

Rule No. 255

Like people and let them know it.

—ROBERT CAPA
PHOTOGRAPHER

Rule No. 256

Work honestly and build, build, build. That's all I can tell you.

—J. R. SIMPLOT
AGRIBUSINESS MAGNATE/
BILLIONAIRE

Rule No. 257

Sometimes a lie makes life more bearable.

—WALTER MOSLEY
WRITER

Rule No. 258

It's possible to own too much. A man with one watch knows what time it is; a man with two watches is never quite sure.

—LEE SEGALL
BUSINESSMAN

Rule No. 259

In all forms of strategy, it is necessary to maintain the combat stance in everyday life and to make your everyday stance your combat stance.

—MIYAMOTO MUSASHI
SWORDSMAN/SAMURAI

Rule No. 260

Don't bunt. Aim out of the ball park. Aim for the company of immortals.

—DAVID OGILVY
ADVERTISING EXECUTIVE

Rule No. 261

Risk! Risk anything! Care no more for the opinion of others, for those voices. Do the hardest thing on earth for you. Act for yourself. Face the truth.

—KATHERINE
MANSFIELD
WRITER

Rule No. 262

Work seriously and steadily. I don't even think geniuses can get good right away.

—TANAKA YUKIO
MUSICIAN

Rule No. 263

Keep looking tanned, live in an elegant building (even if you're in the cellar), be seen in smart restaurants (even if you nurse one drink), and if you borrow, borrow big.

—ARISTOTLE ONASSIS
BUSINESSMAN, ON THE
SECRET OF SUCCESS

Rule No. 264

Don't accept your dog's admiration as conclusive evidence that you are wonderful.

—ANN LANDERS
ADVICE COLUMNIST

Rule No. 265

If a man can beat you, walk him.

—Satchel Paige
BASEBALL PLAYER

Rule No. 266

Never trust a computer you can't throw out a window.

—Steve Wozniak
COMPUTER ENGINEER

Rule No. 267

Everyone at a party is uncomfortable. Knowing that makes me more comfortable.

—GARRY SHANDLING
COMEDIAN

Rule No. 268

I urge you to please notice when you are happy, and exclaim or murmur or think at some point, "If this isn't nice, I don't know what is."

—KURT VONNEGUT
WRITER

Rule No. 269

Trust, but verify.

—DAMON RUNYON
WRITER/JOURNALIST

Rule No. 270

Accept certain inalienable truths: Prices will rise. Politicians will philander. You, too, will get old. And when you do, you'll fantasize that when you were young, prices were reasonable, politicians were noble, and children respected their elders.

—MARY SCHMICH
COLUMNIST

Rule No. 271

The best way out is always through.

—ROBERT FROST
POET

Rule No. 272

A passionate interest in what you do is the secret of enjoying life—whether it is helping old people or children, or making cheese or growing earthworms.

—JULIA CHILD
CHEF

Rule No. 273

Forgive your enemies, but never forget their names.

—JOHN F. KENNEDY
STATESMAN

Rule No. 274

Before doing someone a favor, make sure that he isn't a madman.

—Eugène Labiche
PLAYWRIGHT

Rule No. 275

About all you
can do in life is
be who you are.
Some people will
love you for you.
Most will love you
for what you can
do for them, and
some won't like
you at all.

—RITA MAE BROWN
WRITER

Rule No. 276

Illegitimi non carborundum: Don't let the bastards grind you down.

—JOSEPH W. STILLWELL
GENERAL

Rule No. 277

Just because it's automatic doesn't mean it works.

—DANIEL J. BERNSTEIN
MATHEMATICIAN

Rule No. 278

When you're ready
to quit, you're closer
than you think.
There's an old Chinese
saying that I just love,
and I believe it is so
true. It goes like this:
"The temptation to
quit will be greatest
just before you are
about to succeed."

—BOB PARSONS
DIGITAL ENTREPRENEUR

Rule No. 279

Go where the power lies.
You may not like them.
You may abhor them.
But they are who you
must deal with. Any other
course is a waste of time.

—IAIN MACLEOD
POLITICIAN

Rule No. 280

Never forget: We are alive
within mysteries.

—WENDELL BERRY
WRITER/FARMER

Rule No. 281

Quit smoking, and observe posted speed limits. This will improve your odds of getting old enough to be wise.

—BARBARA KINGSOLVER
WRITER

Rule No. 282

Things are almost never clear on Wall Street, or when they are, then it's too late to profit from them.

—PETER LYNCH
INVESTOR

Rule No. 283

Never stand up straight. That's what World War II taught me. Number one, you might be picked for detail. Number two, the Germans have a better shot at you. Even now, I'm in a perpetual crouch so that nobody picks me for extra duties.

—MEL BROOKS
FILM DIRECTOR

Rule No. 284

Think of yourself as on the threshold of unparalleled success. A whole, clear, glorious life lies before you. Achieve! Achieve!

—ANDREW CARNEGIE
INDUSTRIALIST/
PHILANTHROPIST

Rule No. 285

There is no useful rule without an exception.

—THOMAS FULLER
PHYSICIAN

Rule No. 286

You can discover what your enemy fears most by observing the means he uses to frighten you.

—ERIC HOFFER
*LONGSHOREMAN/
PHILOSOPHER*

Rule No. 287

Everything is negotiable.

—MUHAMMAD ALI
BOXER

Rule No. 288

When in danger, ponder. When in trouble, delegate. And when in doubt, mumble.

—JAMES BOREN
*FOUNDER AND PRESIDENT
OF NATAPROBU, THE
NATIONAL ASSOCIATION OF
PROFESSIONAL BUREAUCRATS*

Rule No. 289

Do what needs to be done, and check to see if it was impossible only after you are done.

—PAUL HAWKEN
ENTREPRENEUR

Rule No. 290

If you only knock long enough and loud enough at the gate you are bound to wake up somebody.

—HENRY WADSWORTH
LONGFELLOW
POET

Rule No. 291

Easy on the mayo!

—MARK BRICKLIN
JOURNALIST

Rule No. 292

There are complete men
and incomplete men.
If you would be a complete
man, put all the strength
of your soul into every
act of your life.

—EUGENIO MARÍA DE
HOSTOS
*EDUCATOR/PHILOSOPHER/
ACTIVIST*

Rule No. 293

Ever notice how "What the hell" is always the right answer?

—MARILYN MONROE
ACTRESS

Rule No. 294

A person who has good thoughts cannot ever be ugly. You can have a wonky nose and a crooked mouth and a double chin and stick-out teeth, but if you have good thoughts they will shine out of your face like sunbeams and you will always look lovely.

—ROALD DAHL
WRITER

Rule No. 295

Never confuse movement with action.

—ERNEST HEMINGWAY
WRITER

Rule No. 296

Regardless of your relationship with your parents, you'll miss them when they're gone from your life.

—MAYA ANGELOU
WRITER

Rule No. 297

Act like you expect to get into the end zone.

—JOE PATERNO
COLLEGE FOOTBALL COACH

Rule No. 298

Do not attack your enemy while he is squatting to defecate.

—**DANIEL OF BECCLES**
*13TH-CENTURY EXPERT ON
ETIQUETTE*

Rule No. 299

When the need arises—
and it does—you must
be able to shoot your own
dog. Don't farm it out—
that doesn't make it nicer,
it makes it worse.

—LAZARUS LONG
*CHARACTER IN WRITER
ROBERT A. HEINLEIN'S
"FUTURE HISTORY" SCIENCE
FICTION SERIES*

Rule No. 300

Learn all you can.

—CLASSROOM RULES
*WESTON MIDDLE SCHOOL,
WESTON, OREGON*

Rule No. 301

Sometimes when you sacrifice something precious, you're not really losing it. You're just passing it on to somebody else.

—MITCH ALBOM
WRITER

Rule No. 302

If you are planning on doing business with someone again, don't be too tough in the negotiations. If you're going to skin a cat, don't keep it as a house cat.

—MARVIN S. LEVIN
FINANCIER

Rule No. 303

It is useless to put
on your brakes when
you're upside down.
—PAUL NEWMAN
ACTOR

Rule No. 304

The thing that's
important to know
is that you never know.
You're always sort
of feeling your way.
—DIANE ARBUS
PHOTOGRAPHER

Rule No. 305

Remembering that you are going to die is the best way I know to avoid the trap of thinking you have something to lose. You are already naked. There is no reason not to follow your heart.

—STEVE JOBS
APPLE COFOUNDER

Rule No. 306

If you're phony,
they will feel
it in the farthest
row of the arena.
You have to really
care. And you
have to make
yourself care time
and time again.

—TOM PETTY
MUSICIAN

Rule No. 307

I have always adhered to two principles. The first one is to train hard and get in the best possible physical condition. The second is to forget all about the other fellow until you face him in the ring and the bell sounds for the fight.

—ROCKY MARCIANO
BOXER

Rule No. 308

If the only tool you have is a hammer, you tend to see every problem as a nail.

—ABRAHAM MASLOW
PSYCHOLOGIST

Rule No. 309

If you do not expect the unexpected you will not find it, for it is not to be reached by search or trail.

—HERACLEITUS
GREEK PHILOSOPHER

Rule No. 310

It never hurts
for potential
opponents to think
you're more than
a little stupid and
can hardly count
all the money in
your hip pocket,
much less hold
on to it.

—AMARILLO SLIM
(THOMAS ALAN
PRESTON JR.)
POKER PLAYER

Rule No. 311

We're all worm bait waiting
to happen. It's what you do
while you wait that matters.

—KINKY FRIEDMAN
SINGER/WRITER

Rule No. 312

Unless you can watch your
stock holdings decline by
50 percent without becoming
panic-stricken, you should
not be in the stock market.

—WARREN BUFFETT
FINANCIER

Rule No. 313

Live so that you can look any man in the eye and tell him to go to hell.

—ENGINEER WORKING
ON THE PANAMA
CANAL
*QUOTED BY JOHN D.
ROCKEFELLER JR. IN A
SPEECH AT DARTMOUTH
COLLEGE, JUNE 1930*

Rule No. 314

If you never assume importance, you never lose it.

—LAO-TZU
CHINESE PHILOSOPHER

Rule No. 315

If you want to achieve excellence, you can get there today. As of this second, quit doing less-than-excellent work.

—THOMAS WATSON
IBM FOUNDER

Rule No. 316

Don't let other people tell you what you want.

—Pat Riley
BASKETBALL COACH

Rule No. 317

How far you go in life
depends on your being
tender with the young,
compassionate with
the aged, sympathetic
with the striving, and
tolerant of the weak
and the strong. Because
someday in life you will
have been all of these.

—GEORGE
WASHINGTON CARVER
SCIENTIST

Rule No. 318

Take care that you
never spell a word wrong.
Always before you write
a word, consider how
it is spelled, and, if you
do not remember, turn
to a dictionary.

—THOMAS JEFFERSON
*STATESMAN, TO HIS
DAUGHTER MARTHA*

Rule No. 319

Keep a thing happenin' all throughout.

—JOHN COLTRANE
MUSICIAN

Rule No. 320

Never keep up with the Joneses. Drag them down to your level.

—QUENTIN CRISP
WRITER

Rule No. 321

"Know thyself" is a good saying, but not in all situations. In many it is better to say "know others."

—MENANDER
GREEK PLAYWRIGHT

Rule No. 322

Avoid extremes. Forbear resenting injuries so much as you think they deserve.

—BENJAMIN FRANKLIN
STATESMAN

Rule No. 323

The world only exists in your eyes. . . . You can make it as big or as small as you want.

—F. SCOTT FITZGERALD
WRITER

Rule No. 324

You can't live a
perfect day without
doing something
for someone who
will never be able
to repay you.

—JOHN WOODEN
COLLEGE BASKETBALL COACH

Rule No. 325

If you aren't cute,
you may as well
be clever.

—DAVID SEDARIS
WRITER

Rule No. 326

Any time you have an opportunity to make a difference in this world and you don't, then you are wasting your time on Earth.

—ROBERTO CLEMENTE
BASEBALL PLAYER

Rule No. 327

You never really learn much
from hearing yourself talk.

—GEORGE CLOONEY
ACTOR

Rule No. 328

Three meals a day.
Work hard. Keep yourself
clean. Get enough sleep.
What else is there?

—ANTONIO PIERRO
WORLD WAR I VETERAN

Rule No. 329

Let no one who has the slightest desire to live in peace and quietness be tempted, under any circumstances, to enter upon the chivalrous task of trying to correct a popular error.

—WILLIAM THOMS
DEPUTY LIBRARIAN FOR THE HOUSE OF LORDS

Rule No. 330

Instead of loving
your enemies,
treat your friends
a little better.

—ED HOWE
JOURNALIST

Rule No. 331

Do not make
the mistake of
trying to revisit
a memory.

—ROD STEIGER
ACTOR

Rule No. 332

If you don't do
it excellently,
don't do it at all.
Because if it's not
excellent, it won't
be profitable or
fun, and if you're
not in business for
fun or profit, what
the hell are you
doing there?

—ROBERT TOWNSEND
BUSINESSMAN

Rule No. 333

Seek simplicity and distrust it.

—Alfred North Whitehead
PHILOSOPHER

Rule No. 334

Eighteen holes of match play will teach you more about your foe than 18 years of dealing with him across a desk.

—Grantland Rice
SPORTSWRITER, ON THE VIRTUES OF GOLF

Rule No. 335

The greatest mistake you can make in life is to be continually fearing you will make one.

—ELBERT G. HUBBARD
WRITER

Rule No. 336

My mother taught me
a lot of things. The first
thing that comes to mind
is: Don't take any s#!%
off anyone, ever. When
I was a little kid, we moved
constantly. Bully picks
on you in the new place?
Don't ever take any s#!%
off anyone, ever. Eloquent
and right.

—JOHNNY DEPP
ACTOR

Rule No. 337

Trust your instincts. Your mistakes might as well be your own instead of someone else's.

—BILLY WILDER
FILM DIRECTOR

Rule No. 338

We know what happens to people who stay in the middle of the road. They get run over.

—ANEURIN BEVAN
POLITICIAN

Rule No. 339

If two friends ask
you to be judge in
a dispute, don't
accept, because
you will lose one
friend; on the
other hand, if two
strangers come
with the same
request, accept,
because you will
gain one friend.

—SAINT AUGUSTINE
BISHOP

Rule No. 340

Laugh at yourself first before anyone else can.

—ELSA MAXWELL
SOCIALITE

Rule No. 341

Always be sincere, even if you don't mean it.

—HARRY S. TRUMAN
STATESMAN

Rule No. 342

Reserve your right to think, for even to think wrongly is better than not to think at all.

—HYPATIA
*GREEK PHILOSOPHER/
SCHOLAR/TEACHER*

Rule No. 343

Don't let your hearts grow numb. Stay alert.

—ALBERT SCHWEITZER
*HUMANITARIAN/
PHILOSOPHER*

Rule No. 344

Love one another and you will be happy. It's as simple and as difficult as that.

—MICHAEL LEUNIG
CARTOONIST

Rule No. 345

The important thing is to sit down at the table and talk. Some things are just easier to say across the remains of a shared meal.

—JESSICA B. HARRIS
COOKBOOK WRITER

Rule No. 346

You must remember always to give, of everything you have. You must give foolishly even. You must be extravagant. You must give to all who come into your life. Then nothing and no one shall have power to cheat you of anything, for if you give to a thief, he cannot steal from you, and he himself is then no longer a thief. And the more you give, the more you will have to give.

—WILLIAM SAROYAN
WRITER

Rule No. 347

Consider, when you are enraged at any one, what you would probably think if he should die during the dispute.

—LUCIUS ANNAEUS
SENECA
*ROMAN PHILOSOPHER/
STATESMAN*

Rule No. 348

Nobody can give you freedom. Nobody can give you equality or justice or anything. If you are a man, you take it.

—MALCOLM X
RELIGIOUS LEADER/ACTIVIST

Rule No. 349

I don't know why we are here, but I'm pretty sure that it is not in order to enjoy ourselves.

—LUDWIG WITTGENSTEIN
PHILOSOPHER

Rule No. 350

We are here on Earth
to fart around. Don't
let anybody tell you
any different.
                    —KURT VONNEGUT
                    WRITER

Rule No. 351

Never do anything
against conscience
even if the state
demands it.
                    —ALBERT EINSTEIN
                    PHYSICIST

Rule No. 352

When making a decision
of minor importance, I have
always found it advantageous
to consider all the pros
and cons. In vital matters,
however, such as the choice
of a mate or profession,
decisions should come
from the unconscious, from
somewhere within ourselves.
In the important decisions of
our personal lives we should
be governed by the deep
inner needs of our nature.

—SIGMUND FREUD
PSYCHIATRIST

Rule No. 353

Trust your gut.

—BARBARA WALTERS
BROADCAST JOURNALIST

Rule No. 354

You don't try. That's very important: not to try, either for Cadillacs, creation or immortality. You wait, and if nothing happens, you wait some more.

—CHARLES BUKOWSKI
WRITER

Rule No. 355

A man who gives a good account of himself is probably lying, since any life when viewed from the inside is simply a series of defeats.

—GEORGE ORWELL
WRITER

Rule No. 356

Talk is cheap.
Show me the code.

—LINUS TORVALDS
SOFTWARE ENGINEER

Rule No. 357

One should always play fairly—
when one has the winning cards.

—OSCAR WILDE
WRITER

Rule No. 358

Make three correct guesses consecutively and you will establish a reputation as an expert.

—LAWRENCE J. PETER
BUSINESS WRITER

Rule No. 359

If you're about to get into a fight, and you know for sure you're going to fight, make sure you punch first.

—Vincent Lecavalier
HOCKEY PLAYER

Rule No. 360

Nobody is as powerful as we make them out to be.

—ALICE WALKER
WRITER

Rule No. 361

We should never lose an occasion. Opportunity is more powerful even than conquerors and prophets.

—BENJAMIN DISRAELI
STATESMAN

Rule No. 362

Call home at least once a week.

—JOHN GRISHAM
WRITER

Rule No. 363

It is better to be approximately right than precisely wrong.

—WARREN BUFFETT
FINANCIER

Rule No. 364

You are young, and have the world before you. Stoop as you go through it, and you will miss many hard thumps.

—Cotton Mather
MINISTER/WRITER,
GIVING ADVICE TO
BENJAMIN FRANKLIN

Rule No. 365

If you do not hope, you will not find what is beyond your hopes.

—CLEMENT OF
ALEXANDRIA
*PATRON SAINT OF THE
UNIVERSAL CATHOLIC
CHURCH*

Rule No. 366

Everybody's their own kind of a damn fool. I'll bet even you think now and then of opportunities missed and think that you could have done perhaps better? I'm full of regrets. Piles and piles of them, but you must not let that bother you. You'd just shoot yourself, which would be nice, but it doesn't pay out. What's the point? So if you can find something to do the way I did, then it keeps you alive. That's the reason I'm alive and active at 85 with lots of work and traveling all over the place. I'll work until I drop, which will be a long time from now.

—PHILIP JOHNSON
ARCHITECT

Rule No. 367

Everything considered, work is less boring than amusing oneself.

—CHARLES BAUDELAIRE
POET

Rule No. 368

Confession may be good for the soul, but it is bad for the reputation.

—THOMAS R. DEWAR
DISTILLER

Rule No. 369

Save yourself several thousand dollars and start flossing like a maniac now.

—Callie Khouri
SCREENWRITER/DIRECTOR

Rule No. 370

You're not supposed to understand everything.

—ROD STEIGER
ACTOR

Rule No. 371

You should always ask yourself what would happen if everyone did what you are doing.

—JEAN-PAUL SARTRE
PHILOSOPHER/WRITER

Rule No. 372

The closer you look at something, the more complex it seems to be.

—Vint Cerf
COMPUTER ENGINEER

Rule No. 373

If only you could
sense how important
you are to the lives
of those you meet;
how important you
can be to people
you may never even
dream of. There is
something of yourself
that you leave at
every meeting with
another person.

—MR. ROGERS
(FRED ROGERS)
CHILDREN'S SHOW HOST

Rule No. 374

Take the course opposite
to custom and you will
almost always do well.

—JEAN-JACQUES
ROUSSEAU
PHILOSOPHER

Rule No. 375

Don't fear god,
Don't worry about death;
What is good is easy
 to get, and
What is terrible is easy
 to endure.

—EPICURUS
ROMAN PHILOSOPHER

Rule No. 376

Don't hitch your wagon to a falling star.

— **JUDGE JUDY
(JUDY SHEINDLIN)**
JURIST/TV SHOW HOST

Rule No. 377

Never think that you're not good enough yourself. A man should never think that. My belief is that in life people will take you at your own reckoning.

—ISAAC ASIMOV
WRITER

Rule No. 378

The great secret of success is to go through life as a man who never gets used up.

—ALBERT SCHWEITZER
HUMANITARIAN/ PHILOSOPHER

Rule No. 379

Any worthwhile expedition can be planned on the back of an envelope.

—HAROLD W. TILMAN
MOUNTAINEER/EXPLORER

Rule No. 380

One thing is certain in business. You and everyone around you will make mistakes.

—RICHARD BRANSON
ENTREPRENEUR

Rule No. 381

The world would never amount to a hill of beans if people didn't use their imaginations to think of the impossible.

—PETE SEEGER
FOLKSINGER

Rule No. 382

Life is bristling with thorns, and I know no other remedy than to cultivate one's garden.

—Voltaire (François-Marie Arouet)
PHILOSOPHER/WRITER

Rule No. 383

Either move
or be moved.

—COLIN POWELL
GENERAL/STATESMAN

Rule No. 384

All you need is
love. But a little
chocolate now and
then doesn't hurt.

—CHARLES M. SCHULZ
CARTOONIST

Rule No. 385

Never regret. If it's good, it's wonderful. If it's bad, it's experience.

—Victoria Holt
(Eleanor Hibbert)
WRITER

Rule No. 386

There's always a reason to smile. Find it.

—Bob Parsons
DIGITAL ENTREPRENEUR

Rule No. 387

Do not draw the conclusion from your apprentice studies that you have nothing left to learn, but rather that you have infinitely more to learn.

—BLAISE PASCAL
*MATHEMATICIAN/
PHILOSOPHER*

Rule No. 388

Fall down, make a mess, break something occasionally. And remember that the story is never over.

—CONAN O'BRIEN
TALK SHOW HOST/COMEDIAN

Rule No. 389

Beware the man of one book.

—THOMAS AQUINAS
PHILOSOPHER/THEOLOGIAN

Rule No. 390

There is much pleasure to be gained from useless knowledge.

—BERTRAND RUSSELL
*MATHEMATICIAN/
PHILOSOPHER*

Rule No. 391

If you don't get too emotional when they like you, you will be less likely to get too emotional when they don't.

—GEORGE ABBOTT
THEATER DIRECTOR/
PRODUCER/PLAYWRIGHT

Rule No. 392

Do the thing you fear most and the death of fear is certain.

—MARK TWAIN
WRITER

Rule No. 393

Never grocery shop on an empty stomach.

—VICTOR J. BOSCHINI
COLLEGE ADMINISTRATOR

Rule No. 394

If only we'd stop trying to be happy we'd have a pretty good time.

—EDITH WHARTON
WRITER

Rule No. 395

Don't give advice, it will come back and bite you in the ass.

—ELLEN DEGENERES
COMEDIAN/TALK SHOW HOST

Rule No. 396

Why not seize the pleasure at once? How often is happiness destroyed by preparation, foolish preparation!

—JANE AUSTEN
WRITER

Rule No. 397

The teachers are everywhere. What is wanted is a learner.

—WENDELL BERRY
WRITER/FARMER

Rule No. 398

Nobody should give a shit about an actor's opinion on politics.

—JAMES CAAN
ACTOR

Rule No. 399

Do not be too moral. You may cheat yourself out of much life so.

—HENRY DAVID
THOREAU
TRANSCENDENTALIST

Rule No. 400

If you make every game a life-and-death proposition, you're going to have problems. For one thing, you'll be dead a lot.

—DEAN SMITH
COLLEGE BASKETBALL COACH

Rule No. 401

It always seems impossible, until it is done.

—NELSON MANDELA
STATESMAN

Rule No. 402

Once a guy starts wearing silk pajamas, it's hard to get up early.

—EDDIE ARCARO
JOCKEY

Rule No. 403

Sing the melody line you hear in your own head.

—BONO
MUSICIAN/ACTIVIST

Rule No. 404

A superior pilot uses his superior judgment to avoid situations which require the use of his superior skill.

—FRANK BORMAN
ASTRONAUT

Rule No. 405

You can overcome anything if you don't bellyache.

—BERNARD BARUCH
FINANCIER

Rule No. 406

Your assumptions
are your windows
on the world.
Scrub them off
every once in a
while or the light
won't come in.

—ALAN ALDA
ACTOR

Rule No. 407

A life directed chiefly
toward fulfillment of
personal desires sooner
or later *always* leads
to bitter disappointment.

—ALBERT EINSTEIN
PHYSICIST

Rule No. 408

Beware of over-great
pleasure in being popular
or even beloved.

—MARGARET FULLER
JOURNALIST/ACTIVIST

Rule No. 409

If people sat outside and looked at the stars each night, I'll bet they'd live a lot differently.

—BILL WATTERSON
CARTOONIST

Rule No. 410

Trust uncertainty, to bring you to clarity.

—JOANNA SWANGER
PROFESSOR

Rule No. 411

I never try to tell anybody else what to do, number one. And number two, I think that's what the individual is all about. Each one of us has something to contribute. . . . Each one possesses exactly what each one is working out, and what each one works out relates to their particular set of circumstances of any one day, or any one place around the world.

—R. BUCKMINSTER FULLER
ARCHITECT/DESIGNER/INVENTOR

Rule No. 412

Pray for the dead and fight like hell for the living.

—MOTHER JONES
(MARY HARRIS JONES)
ACTIVIST

Rule No. 413

Eighty percent of the people who hear [your troubles] don't care and the other twenty percent are glad you're having them.

—TOMMY LASORDA
BASEBALL MANAGER

Rule No. 414

First learn the meaning of what you say, and then speak.

—EPICTETUS
ROMAN PHILOSOPHER

Rule No. 415

Never use a metaphor, simile, or other figure of speech which you are used to seeing in print. Never use a long word where a short one will do. If it is possible to cut a word out, always cut it out. Never use the passive voice where you can use the active. Never use a foreign phrase, a scientific word, or a jargon word if you can think of an everyday English equivalent. Break any of these rules sooner than say anything outright barbarous.

—GEORGE ORWELL
WRITER

Rule No. 416

Don't despair, not even over the fact that you don't despair.

—**FRANZ KAFKA**
WRITER

Rule No. 417

Don't wait until the time or the market is just right to start investing— start now. The best time to plant an oak tree was twenty years ago— the second best time is now.

—JAMES STOWERS JR.
FINANCIER

Rule No. 418

Find things that shine and move toward them.

—MIA FARROW
ACTRESS

Rule No. 419

Go to the edge of the cliff and jump off. Build your wings on the way down.

—RAY BRADBURY
WRITER

Rule No. 420

Learn what pitch you can hit good; then wait for that pitch.

—WEE WILLIE KEELER
BASEBALL PLAYER

Rule No. 421

Get into the game!

—HELEN THOMAS
JOURNALIST

Rule No. 422

Read at every wait; read
at all hours; read within
leisure; read in times
of labor; read as one goes
in; read as one goes out.
The task of the educated
mind is simply put: read
to lead.

—Marcus Tullius
Cicero
*ROMAN PHILOSOPHER/
STATESMAN*

Rule No. 423

Don't hit at all if it is honorably possible to avoid hitting; but never hit softly.

—THEODORE
ROOSEVELT
STATESMAN

Rule No. 424

Do your homework all
of your life.

—MURIEL SIEBERT
BUSINESSWOMAN

Rule No. 425

If you want to have good
ideas you must have
many ideas. Most of them
will be wrong, and what
you have to learn is which
ones to throw away.

—LINUS PAULING
CHEMIST

Rule No. 426

It's not enough to swing at the ball. You've got to loosen your girdle and really let the ball have it.

—BABE DIDRIKSON
ZAHARIAS
GOLFER

Rule No. 427

Don't start an argument with somebody who has a microphone when you don't. They'll make you look like chopped liver.

—HARLAN ELLISON
WRITER

Rule No. 428

Remember, there is a big difference between kneeling down and bending over.

—FRANK ZAPPA
MUSICIAN

Rule No. 429

Always avoid meetings with time-wasting morons.

—SCOTT ADAMS
CARTOONIST

Rule No. 430

Invest at least as much time and effort in choosing a new stock as you would in choosing a new refrigerator.

—PETER LYNCH
INVESTOR

Rule No. 431

If I may lift a line from a die-hard whose identity is lost in the shuffle, "I'd rather be strongly wrong than weakly right."

—TALLULAH BANKHEAD
ACTRESS

Rule No. 432

Don't sidestep suffering. You have to go through it to get where you're going.

—KATHERINE ANNE PORTER
WRITER

Rule No. 433

Be helpful, even if it compromises you.

—JEAN COCTEAU
WRITER/FILMMAKER

Rule No. 434

Be thankful for what you have; you'll end up having more. If you concentrate on what you don't have, you will never, ever have enough.

—OPRAH WINFREY
MEDIA MAGNATE

Rule No. 435

Yes, speak softly and carry a big stick. But don't mumble. And don't swing the stick.

—MARK BRICKLIN
JOURNALIST

Rule No. 436

If you can't change your fate, change your attitude.

—AMY TAN
WRITER

Rule No. 437

Never turn your back on a threatened danger and try to run away from it. If you do that, you will double the danger. But if you meet it promptly and without flinching, you will reduce the danger by half. Never run away from anything. Never!

—WINSTON CHURCHILL
STATESMAN

Rule No. 438

Just play every hand—you can't miss them all.

—SAMMY FARHA
POKER PLAYER

Rule No. 439

Always praise 'em before you hit 'em.

—ROGER STONE
*CONSULTANT/
POLITICAL LOBBYIST*

Rule No. 440

Happiness is a gift and the trick is not to expect it, but to delight in it when it comes.

—CHARLES DICKENS
WRITER

Rule No. 441

This is very important—to take leisure time. Pace is the essence. Without stopping entirely and doing nothing at all for great periods, you're gonna lose everything. Whether you're an actor, anything, a housewife . . . there has to be great pauses between highs, where you do nothing at all. You just lay on a bed and stare at the ceiling. This is very, very important . . . just to do nothing at all, very, very important.

—CHARLES BUKOWSKI
WRITER

Rule No. 442

Always leave them laughing when you say good-bye.

—GEORGE M. COHAN
ENTERTAINER

Rule No. 443

If you always do what interests you, at least one person is pleased.

—KATHARINE HEPBURN
ACTRESS

Rule No. 444

Live by yes and no—
yes to everything good,
no to everything bad.

—**WILLIAM JAMES**
PSYCHOLOGIST/PHILOSOPHER

Rule No. 445

Wherever you go, go with all your heart.

—**CONFUCIUS**
PHILOSOPHER

Rule No. 446

Never be late. When you're late, what you're saying is that your time is more important than the other person's time. That's pretty egotistical.

—ALICE COOPER
MUSICIAN

Rule No. 447

It's no good running a pig farm badly for thirty years while saying, "Really, I was meant to be a ballet dancer." By that time, pigs will be your style.

—QUENTIN CRISP
WRITER

Rule No. 448

Be bold. If you're going
to make an error, make
a doozey, and don't
be afraid to hit the ball.

—BILLIE JEAN KING
TENNIS PLAYER

Rule No. 449

Never explain—your
friends do not need it,
and your enemies will
not believe you anyway.

—ELBERT G. HUBBARD
WRITER

Rule No. 450

You've got to learn
your instrument.
Then, you practice,
practice, practice.
And then, when you
finally get up there on
the bandstand, forget
all that and just wail.

—CHARLIE PARKER
MUSICIAN

Rule No. 451

When you get to the end of your rope— tie a knot in it and hang on.

—**FRANKLIN D. ROOSEVELT**
STATESMAN

Rule No. 452

What you spend years building may be destroyed overnight; build it anyway.

—**MOTHER TERESA**
HUMANITARIAN

Rule No. 453

Never miss a good chance to shut up.

—WILL ROGERS
HUMORIST

Rule No. 454

Only a fool holds out for the top dollar.

—JOSEPH P. KENNEDY
BUSINESSMAN

Rule No. 455

Always forgive your enemies— nothing annoys them so much.

—Oscar Wilde
WRITER

Rule No. 456

Anything you're rigid about, sooner or later, the rug is going to get pulled out from under you.

—ALAN ARKIN
ACTOR

Rule No. 457

Never go for the punch line. There might be something funnier on the way.

—JERRY STILLER
COMEDIAN

Rule No. 458

Thou shalt not have many who know of thy love affair.

—ANDREAS
CAPELLANUS
CLERIC

Rule No. 459

You need to be absolutely paranoid about the currency of your knowledge and ask yourself every day: Am I really up to speed? Or am I stagnating intellectually, faking it or even worse, falling behind? Am I still learning? Or am I just doing the same stuff on a different day? Or as Otis Redding sings, "Sitting on the dock of the bay watching the tide roll away."

—DAVID L. CALHOUN
BUSINESSMAN

Rule No. 460

Buy a steak for a player on another club after the game, but don't even speak to him on the field. Get out there and beat them to death.

—LEO DUROCHER
BASEBALL MANAGER

Rule No. 461

Whatever you are, be a good one.

—ABRAHAM LINCOLN
STATESMAN

Rule No. 462

Stare. It is the way to educate your eye, and more. Stare, pry, listen, eavesdrop. Die knowing something. You are not here long.

—**WALKER EVANS**
PHOTOGRAPHER

Rule No. 463

Those who don't believe in magic will never find it.

—ROALD DAHL
WRITER

Rule No. 464

Bend down once in a while and smell a flower.

—RUSSELL BAKER
COLUMNIST

<u>Rule(s) No. 465</u>

Three of the four most important lessons I ever learned in life came from my stepdad:

1. The only person you can count on in life is yourself.

2. You can't be happy with someone else until you're happy with yourself.

3. Don't lie and don't break your word.

(Note: The fourth lesson came from my Aunt Jen, who taught me, "If you're interested in a girl, always meet her mom because all girls end up eventually turning into their moms, with no exceptions.")

—BILL SIMMONS
SPORTSWRITER

Rule No. 466

Believe in this world— that there is meaning behind everything.

—VIVEKANANDA
BENGALI MYSTIC

Rule No. 467

Do not keep saying to yourself, if you can possibly avoid it, "But how can it be like that?" because you will get "down the drain," into a blind alley from which nobody has yet escaped. Nobody knows how it can be like that.

—RICHARD FEYNMAN
PHYSICIST

Rule No. 468

Never sleep with anyone
who has more trouble or
less money than you have.

—DAVID BROWN
FILM PRODUCER

Rule No. 469

The best way to get on
in the world is to make
people believe it's to their
advantage to help you.

—JEAN DE LA BRUYÈRE
WRITER/MORALIST

Rule No. 470

If you want to kill any idea in the world, get a committee working on it.

—CHARLES F. KETTERING
ENGINEER/INVENTOR

Rule No. 471

If you don't risk anything, you risk even more.

—ERICA JONG
WRITER

Rule No. 472

It's morally wrong to let a sucker keep money.

—CANADA BILL JONES
CARDSHARP

Rule No. 473

If you challenge your own,
you won't be so quick
to accept the unchallenged
assumptions of others.
You'll be a lot less likely
to be caught up in bias or
prejudice or be influenced
by people who ask you to
hand over your brains, your
soul, or your money because
they have everything all
figured out for you.

—ALAN ALDA
ACTOR

Rule No. 474

Chase after the truth like all hell and you'll free yourself, even though you never touch its coat tails.

—CLARENCE DARROW
LAWYER

Rule No. 475

"A cucumber is bitter."
Throw it away.
"There are briars
in the road." Turn
aside from them.
This is enough. Do
not add, "And why
were such things
made in the world?"

—MARCUS AURELIUS
ROMAN EMPEROR

Rule No. 476

Never say anything on the phone that you wouldn't want your mother to hear at the trial.

—SYDNEY BIDDLE
BARROWS
*MADAM, UPSCALE
ESCORT SERVICE*

Rule No. 477

You don't have to rush down the hill. You can walk down.

—CLINT EASTWOOD
FILM DIRECTOR/ACTOR

Rule No. 478

If people don't occasionally walk away from you shaking their heads, you're doing something wrong.

—JOHN GIERACH
FLY FISHERMAN

Rule No. 479

Read everything.

—JIM ROGERS
FINANCIER

Rule No. 480

Beware of irony when making judgments. Of all the dispositions of the mind, irony is the least intelligent.

—CHARLES-AUGUSTIN
SAINTE-BEUVE
LITERARY CRITIC

Rule No. 481

The nearest way to glory—
a shortcut, as it were—
is to strive to be what you
wish to be thought to be.

—SOCRATES
PHILOSOPHER

Rule No. 482

Just remember, we're all
in this alone.

—JANE WAGNER
WRITER/DIRECTOR

Rule No. 483

Don't give your opinions about Art and the Purpose of Life. They are of little interest and, anyway, you can't express them.

—EVELYN WAUGH
WRITER

Rule No. 484

Think in the morning. Act in the noon. Eat in the evening. Sleep in the night.

—WILLIAM BLAKE
POET

Rule No. 485

Never hurry and never worry.

—E. B. WHITE
WRITER

Rule No. 486

It is good to love many things, for therein lies the true strength, and whosoever loves much performs much, and can accomplish much, and what is done in love is well done.

—VINCENT VAN GOGH
PAINTER

Rule No. 487

If your desk isn't covered, you probably aren't doing your job.

—HAROLD S. GENEEN
BUSINESSMAN

Rule No. 488

One thing you cannot afford to do—that's to feel sorry for yourself.

—WOODY HAYES
COLLEGE FOOTBALL COACH

Rule No. 489

Think for yourself and question authority.

—TIMOTHY LEARY
PROFESSOR/
COUNTERCULTURE LEADER

Rule No. 490

If you wish to win a man's heart, allow him to confute you.

—BENJAMIN DISRAELI
STATESMAN

Rule No. 491

Sandwich every bit of criticism between two heavy layers of praise.

—MARY KAY ASH
BUSINESSWOMAN

Rule No. 492

There are no rules for good photographs, there are only good photographs.

—ANSEL ADAMS
PHOTOGRAPHER

Rule No. 493

Never turn your back on a friend.

—ALFRED HITCHCOCK
FILM DIRECTOR

Rule No. 494

You're never as good
as everyone tells you when
you win, and you're never
as bad as they say when
you lose.

—LOU HOLTZ
COLLEGE FOOTBALL COACH

Rule No. 495

Do not bite at the bait
of pleasure until you know
there is no hook beneath it.

—THOMAS JEFFERSON
STATESMAN

Rule No. 496

I once complained
to my father that
I didn't seem to be
able to do things
the same way other
people did. Dad's
advice? "Margo,
don't be a sheep.
People hate sheep.
They eat sheep."

—MARGO KAUFMAN
WRITER

Rule No. 497

When a door is hard to open, and if nothing else works, sometimes you just have to rear back and kick it open.

—MURIEL SIEBERT
BUSINESSWOMAN

Rule No. 498

Make love when you can. It's good for you.

—KURT VONNEGUT
WRITER

Rule No. 499

It's better to be a pirate than to join the navy.

—STEVE JOBS
APPLE COFOUNDER

Rule No. 500

Attack, always attack.

—GEORGE S. PATTON
GENERAL

Rule(s) No. 501

Having served on various committees, I have drawn up a list of rules:

1. Never arrive on time; this stamps you as a beginner.

2. Don't say anything until the meeting is half over; this stamps you as being wise.

3. Be as vague as possible; this avoids irritating the others.

4. When in doubt, suggest that a subcommittee be appointed.

5. Be the first one to move for adjournment; this will make you popular; it's what everyone is waiting for.

—HENRY CHAPMAN
POLITICIAN

Rule No. 502

Never trust a man who speaks well of everybody.

—JOHN CHURTON
COLLINS
WRITER

Rule No. 503

Underpromise and overdeliver.

—ROBIN LI
BUSINESSMAN

Rule No. 504

It is a mistake to look too far ahead. The chain of destiny can only be grasped one link at a time.

—WINSTON CHURCHILL
STATESMAN

Rule No. 505

You can do anything you want to do as long as you keep a good attitude and keep working at it. But the second you give up, you're screwed.

—DOLLY PARTON
SINGER

Rule No. 506

Watch out for emergencies. They are your big chance.

—FRITZ REINER
CONDUCTOR

Rule No. 507

When looking at any significant work of art, remember that a more significant one probably has had to be sacrificed.

—PAUL KLEE
ARTIST

Rule No. 508

Courage is more exhilarating than fear, and in the long run it is easier.

—ELEANOR ROOSEVELT
POLITICIAN/ACTIVIST

Rule No. 509

The race is not always to the swift, nor the battle to the strong, but that's the way to bet.

—DAMON RUNYON
WRITER/JOURNALIST

Rule No. 510

Whatever terrible thing is going on, it's going on until you find out that it's not. So get to that part as quickly as possible.

—MICHAEL J. FOX
ACTOR

Rule No. 511

Keep your head on straight, don't get emotional, take the heat, and just make sure your clients are smiling.

—SCOTT BORAS
SPORTS AGENT

Rule No. 512

Reflect upon your present blessings—of which every man has many—not on your past misfortunes, of which all men have some.

—CHARLES DICKENS
WRITER

Rule No. 513

There are two kinds of people, those who do the work and those who take the credit. Try to be in the first group; there is less competition there.

—INDIRA GANDHI
STATESWOMAN

Rule No. 514

Let bravery be your choice, but not bravado.

—MENANDER
GREEK PLAYWRIGHT

Rule No. 515

When all else fails, there's always delusion.

—CONAN O'BRIEN
TALK SHOW HOST/COMEDIAN

Rule No. 516

Try to decide how good your hand is at a given moment. Nothing else matters. Nothing!

—DOYLE BRUNSON
POKER PLAYER

Rule No. 517

Avoid people with gold teeth who want to play cards.

—GEORGE CARLIN
COMEDIAN

Rule No. 518

It ain't as bad as you think. It will look better in the morning.

—COLIN POWELL
GENERAL/STATESMAN

Rule No. 519

No matter what you do or where you are, you're going to be missing out on something.

—ALAN ARKIN
ACTOR

Rule No. 520

As you go through life,
you will discover that
more and more of the
subjects you studied
in college are useless,
with the exception of
abnormal psychology.

—MARK BRICKLIN
JOURNALIST

Rule No. 521

It is enough to be able to
do harm, when you have
the power of harming.
Do not rain down damage
on anyone, when you hit
the stars with your head.

—DANIEL OF BECCLES
*13TH-CENTURY EXPERT ON
ETIQUETTE*

Rule(s) No. 522

The classroom rules are:

Be Prompt
Be Prepared
Be Polite

—CLASSROOM RULES
*POSTED BY MRS. LUSK,
PARKER, ARIZONA*

Rule No. 523

It is too difficult to think nobly when one thinks only of earning a living.

—JEAN-JACQUES
ROUSSEAU
PHILOSOPHER

Rule No. 524

Always be the only person who can sign your checks.

—OPRAH WINFREY
MEDIA MAGNATE

Rule No. 525

Remind people that profit is the difference between revenue and expense. This makes you look smart.

—SCOTT ADAMS
CARTOONIST

Rule No. 526

The wind is blowing, adore the wind.

—**Pythagoras**
PHILOSOPHER

Rule No. 527

You've got to have something to eat and a little love in your life. Everything goes smack back to that.

—BILLIE HOLIDAY
SINGER

Rule No. 528

You don't need to wear a necktie if you can hit.

—TED WILLIAMS
BASEBALL PLAYER

Rule No. 529

Cross the river before reviling the crocodile's mother.

—BILL TILMAN
MOUNTAINEER/EXPLORER

Rule No. 530

Don't agonize. Organize.

—**FLORYNCE KENNEDY**
LAWYER/ACTIVIST

Rule No. 531

If you turn the other cheek, you will get a harder blow on it than you got on the first one. This does not always happen, but it is to be expected, and you ought not to complain if it does happen.

—**GEORGE ORWELL**
WRITER

Rule No. 532

Life is to be lived. If you have to support yourself, you had bloody well better find some way that is going to be interesting. And you don't do that by sitting around wondering about yourself.

—KATHARINE HEPBURN
ACTRESS

Rule No. 533

There is a way to look at the past. Don't hide from it. It will not catch you if you don't repeat it.

—PEARL BAILEY
SINGER/ACTRESS

Rule No. 534

Think hard about who you marry. It's the most important decision you will ever make. Devote yourself to your kids. Nothing else is guaranteed to make you happy.

—DAVID BROOKS
COLUMNIST

Rule No. 535

Just rock on and have you a good time.

—DUANE ALLMAN
MUSICIAN

Rule No. 536

Our life is frittered away by detail. . . . Simplify, simplify.

—HENRY DAVID
THOREAU
TRANSCENDENTALIST

Rule No. 537

Never think you've seen the last of anything.

—EUDORA WELTY
WRITER

Rule No. 538

When you are offended at any man's fault, turn to yourself and study your own failings. Then you will forget your anger.

—Epictetus
GREEK PHILOSOPHER

Rule No. 539

You only find out who is swimming naked when the tide goes out.

—WARREN BUFFETT
FINANCIER

Rule No. 540

Most of what matters in your life takes place in your absence.

—SALMAN RUSHDIE
WRITER

Rule No. 541

If you hear that *everybody* is buying a certain stock, ask who is selling.

—JAMES DINES
INVESTMENT ADVISER

Rule No. 542

Never be ashamed to ask for information. The ignorant man will always be ignorant if he hears that by asking he will display ignorance.

—BOOKER T. WASHINGTON
EDUCATOR

Rule No. 543

Almost any man looks better in a dark suit.

—BOB BARKER
GAME SHOW HOST

Rule No. 544

Keep your face to the sunshine and you cannot see the shadow.

—HELEN KELLER
WRITER/ACTIVIST

Rule No. 545

Trade a player a year too early rather than a year too late.

—BRANCH RICKEY
BASEBALL MANAGER

Rule No. 546

Sometimes the questions are complicated and the answers are simple.

—Dr. Seuss
(Theodor Geisel)
WRITER

Rule No. 547

God will protect us, but to make sure, carry a heavy club.

—GYPSY ROSE LEE
BURLESQUE STRIPPER

Rule(s) No. 548

1. Carefully observe oneself and one's situation, carefully observe others, and carefully observe one's environment.

2. Seize the initiative in whatever you undertake.

3. Consider fully, act decisively.

4. Know when to stop.

5. Keep to the middle.

—JIGORO KANO
JUDO MASTER

Rule No. 549

Don't anticipate life;
meet it. When you try
to anticipate, you're being
an idiot, because nobody's
got the brain to outwit
nature. I'm talking here
about patience, about
believing in yourself. I'm
talking here about having
courage to wait. You will
get what you deserve.

—ROD STEIGER
ACTOR

Rule No. 550

If at first you don't succeed, try, try again. Then quit. No use being a damn fool about it.

—W. C. FIELDS
COMEDIAN

Rule No. 551

Treat people as if they were what they ought to be and you will help them become what they are capable of becoming.

—JOHANN WOLFGANG
VON GOETHE
WRITER

Rule No. 552

There is a way to do it better— find it.

—THOMAS A. EDISON
INVENTOR

Rule No. 553

Don't let your mouth write a check that your tail can't cash.

—BO DIDDLEY
MUSICIAN

Rule No. 554

When an old and distinguished person speaks to you, listen to him carefully and with respect—but do not believe him. Never put your trust into anything but your own intellect. Your elder, no matter whether he has gray hair or has lost his hair, no matter whether he is a Nobel laureate—may be wrong.

—LINUS PAULING
CHEMIST

Rule No. 555

The first rule of holes: When you're in one, stop digging.

—MOLLY IVINS
WRITER

Rule No. 556

My daddy said, "When the sun comes up, boy, you get up. When the sun go down, dammit, you go down."

—AL GREEN
SINGER/PREACHER

Rule No. 557

You were born with wings. Why prefer to crawl through life?

—RUMI
PERSIAN POET/MYSTIC

Rule No. 558

In whatever you are doing, failure is an option. But fear is not.

—JAMES CAMERON
FILM DIRECTOR

Rule No. 559

Your problems never cease. They just change.

—PHIL JACKSON
BASKETBALL COACH

Rule No. 560

There is no conclusive evidence of life after death. But there is no evidence of any sort against it. Soon enough you will know. So why fret about it?

—LAZARUS LONG
CHARACTER IN WRITER
ROBERT A. HEINLEIN'S
"FUTURE HISTORY"
SCIENCE FICTION SERIES

Rule No. 561

The best ideas come as jokes. Make your thinking as funny as possible.

—DAVID OGILVY
ADVERTISING EXECUTIVE

Rule No. 562

When you see a snake, never mind where he came from.

—WILLIAM GURNEY
BENHAM
WRITER

Rule No. 563

Don't borrow to buy depreciating assets. Almost every consumer product from an iPod to a sofa is worth less the moment you buy it. You are just paying extra for it with a loan. Borrowing, by the way, means taking out a loan, buying it on installment or using your credit card when you don't have the money to pay off the balance. If you can't afford it, don't buy it.

—DAMON DARLIN
JOURNALIST

Rule No. 564

Always look out for
Number One and be careful
not to step in Number Two.

—RODNEY
DANGERFIELD
COMEDIAN

Rule No. 565

If you read
someone else's
diary, you get
what you deserve.

—DAVID SEDARIS
WRITER

Rule No. 566

If you have an idea, that's good. If you also have an idea as to how to work it out, that's better.

—HENRY FORD
BUSINESSMAN

Rule No. 567

Learn to fail with pride—and do so fast and cleanly. Maximize trial and error—by mastering the error part.

—Nassim
Nicholas Taleb
TRADER/WRITER

Rule No. 568

Nothing in life is "fun for the whole family."

—Jerry Seinfeld
COMEDIAN

Rule No. 569

If you don't know what it is, don't mess with it.

—FATS WALLER
MUSICIAN

Rule No. 570

When Joseph Campbell said to follow your bliss, I'm sure he meant: Don't walk after it, but run. So be prepared to sweat.

—TOM FRESTON
BUSINESSMAN

Rule No. 571

I've learned the glories of laughter. Don't take things too seriously. Celebrate life.

—Luis Haza
VIOLINIST/CONDUCTOR

Rule No. 572

Understand, when you eat meat, that something did die. You have an obligation to value it—not just the sirloin but also all those wonderful tough little bits.

—Anthony Bourdain
CHEF

Rule No. 573

There's no there. That elusive "there" with the job, the beach house, the dream, it's not out there. There is here. It's in you . . . right now.

—BRIAN KENNY
SPORTSCASTER

Rule No. 574

The first and final thing you have to do in this world is to last in it and not be smashed by it.

—ERNEST HEMINGWAY
WRITER

Rule No. 575

Never go out to meet trouble. If you will just sit still, nine cases out of ten someone will intercept it for you.

—CALVIN COOLIDGE
STATESMAN

Rule No. 576

There is no substitute for hard work, for doing well at the job you're in. When I made coffee and Xeroxed and distributed newspapers at ABC News, I thought my life was over. But I did it; I didn't complain. And along the way, I learned a lot, and was ready for the bigger jobs that were around the corner.

—KATIE COURIC
NEWSCASTER

Rule No. 577

You're the only one who's closing your eyes at night. There's no one else who can do it for you.

—James Caan
ACTOR

Rule No. 578

If you can accept loss, you can accept the fact that there's gonna be the big loss. Once you can accept that, you can accept anything.

—Michael J. Fox
ACTOR

Rule No. 579

Sure, luck means a lot in football. Not having a good quarterback is bad luck.

—DON SHULA
FOOTBALL COACH

Rule No. 580

If you want to play a game, go to where it's played and find a way to get in. Things happen when you get in the game.

—CHRIS MATTHEWS
POLITICAL COMMENTATOR

Rule No. 581

Life loves to be taken by the lapels and told: "I am with you, kid. Let's go."

—MAYA ANGELOU
WRITER

Rule No. 582

If you can gain control over 60 percent of the time in your life, you are really successful.

—ROD STEIGER
ACTOR

Rule No. 583

Love what you do. Get good at it. Competence is a rare commodity in this day and age.

—JON STEWART
COMEDIAN/TV SHOW HOST

Rule No. 584

You have to grow from the inside out. None can teach you, none can make you spiritual. There is no other teacher but your own soul.

—Vivekananda
BENGALI MYSTIC

Rule No. 585

Never follow
the crowd.

—**BERNARD BARUCH**
FINANCIER

Rule No. 586

Deplore your mistakes.
Regret them as much
as you like. But don't
really expect to learn
by them.

—**CARY GRANT**
ACTOR

Rule No. 587

The one important thing
I have learned over the
years is the difference
between taking one's work
seriously and taking one's
self seriously. The first is
imperative and the second
is disastrous.

—MARGOT FONTEYN
BALLERINA

Rule No. 588

Try to avoid falling out
with people. The world
is a very small place.

—RICHARD BRANSON
ENTREPRENEUR

Rule No. 589

It's sometimes better
to pretend I don't hear
the sound of somebody
in the nearby woods with
a shotgun.

—DASHIELL HAMMETT
WRITER

Rule No. 590

No matter how sophisticated you may be, a large granite mountain cannot be denied— it speaks in silence to the very core of your being.

—Ansel Adams
PHOTOGRAPHER

Rule No. 591

Always try to rub against money, for if you rub against money long enough, some of it may rub off on you.

—DAMON RUNYON
WRITER/JOURNALIST

Rule No. 592

All you need for a movie is a gun and a girl.

—JEAN-LUC GODARD
FILM DIRECTOR

Rule No. 593

A man ought to get all
he can earn. A man
who knows he's making
money for other people
ought to get some of the
profit he brings in. Don't
make any difference if
it's baseball or a bank
or a vaudeville show.
It's business, I tell you.
There ain't no sentiment
to it. Forget that stuff.

—BABE RUTH
BASEBALL PLAYER

Rule No. 594

Don't compromise yourself. You are all you've got.

—JANIS JOPLIN
SINGER

Rule No. 595

Be willing to make decisions. . . . Don't fall victim to what I call the "ready-aim-aim-aim-aim" syndrome.

—T. BOONE PICKENS
BUSINESSMAN

Rule No. 596

Try to learn to breathe deeply, really to taste food when you eat, and when you sleep really to sleep. Try as much as possible to be wholly alive with all your might, and when you laugh, laugh like hell. And when you get angry, get good and angry. Try to be alive. You will be dead soon enough.

—WILLIAM SAROYAN
WRITER

Rule No. 597

Be optimistic. Always
put on clean underwear
if you're going on a date.

—JACOB M. APPEL
PLAYWRIGHT

Rule No. 598

You must not lose faith in
humanity. Humanity is an
ocean; if a few drops of the
ocean are dirty, the ocean
does not become dirty.

—MOHANDAS K.
GANDHI
STATESMAN

Rule No. 599

Seize the moments of happiness, love and be loved! That is the only reality in the world, all else is folly. It is the one thing we are interested in here.

—LEO TOLSTOY
WRITER

Rule No. 600

Don't ever write anything
you don't like yourself
and if you do like it, don't
take anyone's advice about
changing it. They just
don't know.

—RAYMOND CHANDLER
WRITER

Rule No. 601

The secret of business
is to know something
that nobody else knows.

—ARISTOTLE ONASSIS
BUSINESSMAN

Rule No. 602

Be polite and generous, but don't undervalue yourself. You will be useful, at any rate; you may just as well be happy, while you are about it.

—OLIVER WENDELL HOLMES
PHYSICIAN/WRITER

Rule No. 603

One should respect public opinion insofar as is necessary to avoid starvation and keep out of prison, but anything that goes beyond this is voluntary submission to an unnecessary tyranny.

—BERTRAND RUSSELL
*MATHEMATICIAN/
PHILOSOPHER*

Rule No. 604

The four most expensive words in the English language are "this time it's different."

—JOHN TEMPLETON
INVESTOR

Rule No. 605

Get rid of those terrible jeans that everybody else wears. And wear something different for a change, so you don't just look like a clone.

—VIVIENNE WESTWOOD
FASHION DESIGNER

Rule No. 606

The easiest way to attract a crowd is to let it be known that at a given time and a given place someone is going to attempt something that in the event of failure will mean sudden death.

—HARRY HOUDINI
MAGICIAN

Rule No. 607

Don't forget that you're
a mental being, with
a humongous trillion
gigawatt hard-drive
at your disposal.

—STEPHEN KING
WRITER

Rule No. 608

If the only prayer
you said in your
whole life was
"Thank You,"
that would suffice.

—MEISTER ECKEHART
GERMAN MYSTIC

Rule No. 609

You don't have to be a
fantastic hero to do certain
things—to compete. You
can be just an ordinary
chap, sufficiently motivated
to reach challenging goals.
The intense effort, the
giving of everything you've
got, is a very pleasant
bonus.

—EDMUND HILLARY
EXPLORER

Rule No. 610

Cheer up. You never know— maybe something awful will happen tomorrow.

—JOHN WATERS
FILM DIRECTOR

Rule No. 611

Before you can steal fire from the Gods you gotta be able to get coffee for the director.

—DAVID MAMET
PLAYWRIGHT

Rule No. 612

Don't be afraid to be a fool. Remember, you cannot be both young and wise. Young people who pretend to be wise to the ways of the world are mostly just cynics. Cynicism masquerades as wisdom, but it is the farthest thing from it. Because cynics don't learn anything. Because cynicism is a self-imposed blindness, a rejection of the world because we are afraid it will hurt us or disappoint us. Cynics always say no. But saying yes begins things. Saying yes is how things grow. Saying yes leads to knowledge. "Yes" is for young people. So for as long as you have the strength to, say yes.

—STEPHEN COLBERT
COMEDIAN/TV SHOW HOST

Rule No. 613

Believe it is possible to solve your problem. Tremendous things happen to the believer. Believe the answer will come. It will.

—NORMAN VINCENT PEALE

PASTOR

Rule No. 614

Wear your best for your execution and stand dignified. Your last recourse against randomness is how you act— if you can't control outcomes, you can control the elegance of your behavior. You will always have the last word.

—NASSIM NICHOLAS TALEB
TRADER/WRITER

Rule No. 615

Don't worry about the darkness— turn on the light and the darkness automatically goes.

—DAVID LYNCH
FILM DIRECTOR

Rule No. 616

Listen, if you start
worrying about
the people in the
stands, before too
long you're up in the
stands with them.

—Tommy Lasorda
BASEBALL MANAGER

Rule No. 617

Shh. Listen to
the sounds that
surround you.

—Pete Seeger
FOLKSINGER